WHAT KEANU SAYS

THE UNOFFICIAL COLLECTION

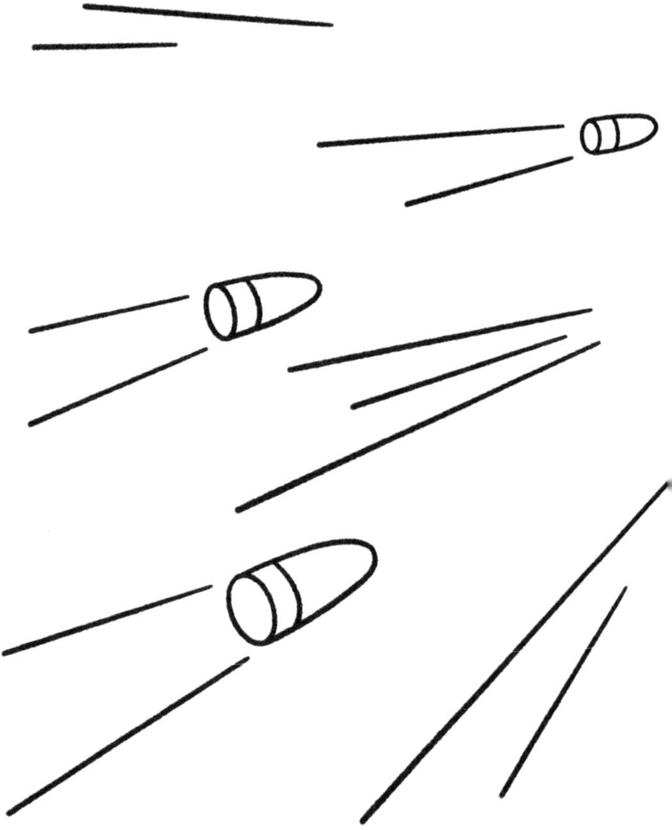

WHAT KEANU SAYS

Quadrille

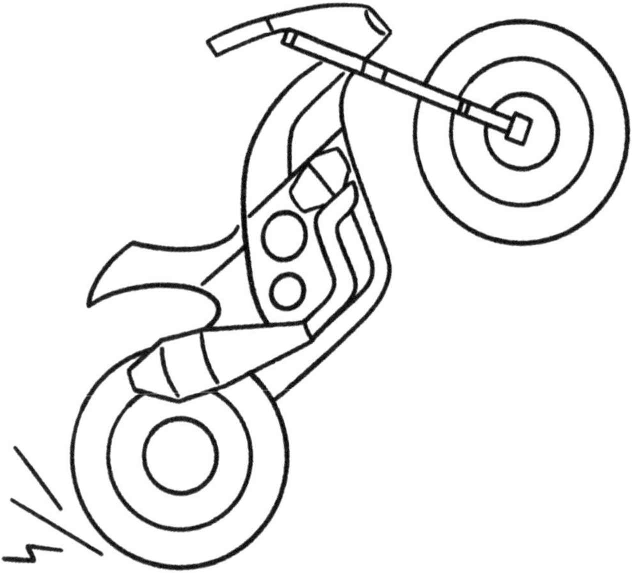

Is Keanu Reeves is an angel sent to Earth, or just Hollywood's coolest dude? Unlike most film stars, he is notorious for his incredible kindness and generosity. He has gifted Harley Davidson motorcycles to his stuntmen and helped complete strangers in their hours of need. And it's not to maintain an image—he hates being called 'nice' and prefers to keep his good deeds private.

While this makes Keanu the perfect sweetheart for romantic movies like *The Lake House* and *Always Be My Maybe*, there are many depths to the actor. He has starred in comedies like *Bill and Ted's Excellent Adventure*, played Hamlet, performed at music festivals and written a graphic novel. However, he is best known as an action man, leading 'gun-fu' movies from *The Matrix* to the *John Wick* franchise. He embraces the fun and exhilaration of these films the same way he rides his motorbike: with freewheeling enjoyment of a life that he knows is all too short and sweet.

Action

Man

"[*The Matrix*] was the most incredible experience of my career."

"[*John Wick*] movies are made for the big screen. We got popcorn—you gotta have popcorn."

"You describe John Wick as a killer and an assassin. I also think of [him] as a widower and someone who's trapped in circumstances that he has no control over."

"I really liked the character.
I liked John's grief,
I liked his will,
I liked his fighting
for his self-agency."

"I have a pretty self-motivated temperament. Even when I was a kid. 'Let's go make something! Let's do something!'"

"A movie is all-hands-on-deck. I love all-hands-on-deck."

“I like fake fights and doing all that kind of stuff.”

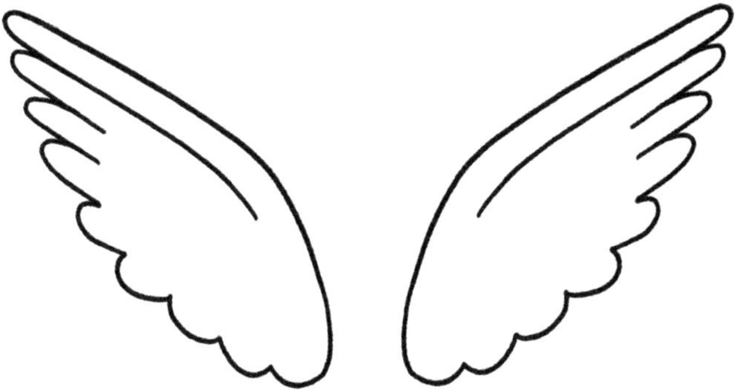

"It's always fun to fly in dreams, isn't it? I'm just glad I have the chance to do it anywhere. It's quite extraordinary."

“For me, motorcycles are my main transport.”

"The physical sensation of riding [a motorbike], the wind, the smell, the sights, the connection to the machine, the living-in-nature. It demands a kind of attention and presentness."

Just

a Normal Guy

"I'm a pretty private person. But I don't have anything to tweet, or say, or anything."

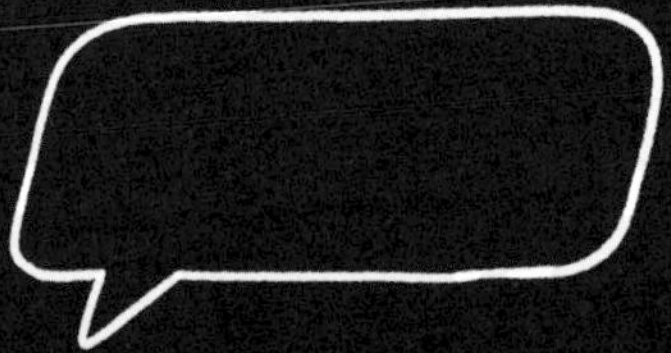

"I'm just in the bell curve of humanity, cruising along where I should be."

"I probably should have taken more advantage [of being a pin-up] but I didn't. You know, I was a little self-conscious about that."

"I have nothing going on! I have no life! It's just going to work and preparation."

"I'm the worst bass player in the whole world. I have no rhythm."

"I was kinda shy in school, but I also had the class-clown element about me. I was removed, but I was involved."

"I don't play stupid. Either it's been a failure on my part to articulate, or my naivete, or ingenuousness."

"I'm just a normal guy, man."

On

Life

"I'm interested in whoever I'm speaking to. I care."

"Even as a kid, I was pretty empathetic."

"If someone comes to you for help [...] you can have a conversation...

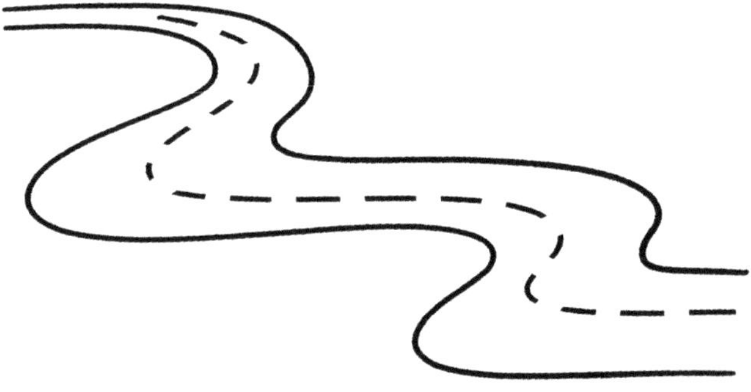

You haven't walked in their shoes, but you know a bit of the road that they've been on."

"I like to read.
I go through phases.
There's always a book."

"I love owning things, I love having stuff. I'm certainly not going to present myself as someone who gives everything away."

"I love traveling. I love new experiences."

"I try not to do anything I don't want to do."

"If you're getting to know me, I guess you could do it through my work."

"Maybe it's because I'm a Virgo; it's in my sign to be hard on myself."

"We can always do more.
There's no ceiling on that.
And you can't do everything.
You can't do it all."

"I think you do all you can for the ones you love."

Playing

Part

the

"I like telling stories, or being part of a story."

"[Storytelling is] asking questions. Looking at the diamond and seeing which ways the light refracts and reflects."

"We're only getting to tell these stories because of the audience. So, thank you."

"There's always a relationship—a drama, a circumstance—in storytelling. But for me, it's cool when a work of art can entertain but also be inspirational or challenging."

“[Acting] is about investigating ‘Why?’, investigating ‘How come?’”

"There have been situations where my relationship with the director has been at odds, I might have been emotionally immature sometimes, I might have shouted a few 'F*cks!'"

"I try to think about what
the creators were going for.
It's their work of art, man.
I try to come to their art
and meet it wherever it is."

"I feel really fortunate in a way, because I knew what I wanted to do, and a lot of kids that age don't. But I had a creative ambition and I did it."

"I still have ambition and hope, and I still wanna do good work and work with people."

"I wanna be 100 years old, but also [make] 100 films."

"I still love acting and I still love the creativity of it."

"For me, acting is very self-involved, especially between projects. Once you get a part, you're liberated."

"It hit me that theater can actually do something, that it's physical and emotional and human...

It's in the heavens and in the earth and it just vibrates through us."

"I tend to throw out a little Shakespeare once in a while [...] it is the most powerful and consuming and freeing at the same time."

"You want to know my favorite role? Mercutio—you know, in *Romeo and Juliet*—'cause he's so full of passion and wisdom and anger."

"My work is play."

"A good day on the set, creating the work, the piece, the collaboration, expression, is a hoot. I love it."

On Love

and

Loss

"Grief and loss, those are things that don't ever go away. They stay with you."

"It's about the love of the person you're grieving for, and any time you can keep company with that fire, it is warm."

"I feel like there's a melancholy [that's] not disappointment, but it's a yearning."

"Grief changes shape, but it never ends."

"When the people you love are gone, you're alone. I miss being a part of their life, and them being a part of mine...

I wonder what the present would be like if they were here—what we might have done together. I miss all the great things that will never be."

"All you can do is hope that grief will be transformed and, instead of feeling pain and confusion, you will be together again in memory."

"There's something, ultimately, about the creative gesture that comes from pain."

"Much of my appreciation of life has come through loss."

"I think thinking about
death is good.
Hopefully it sensitizes [us]
to an appreciation of the
breath we have,
in the relationships
that we have the
potential to have."

Woah

Dude

"What is this quest for immortality?"

"I'm so glad I've hallucinated in my life. I think that's one of the most beautiful things. Isn't it one of the most amazing things?"

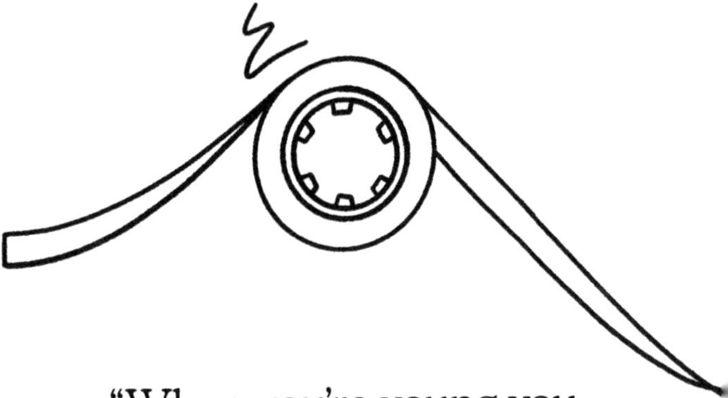

"When you're young you have a big old reel of that tape left, right? And so it appears to revolve slowly…

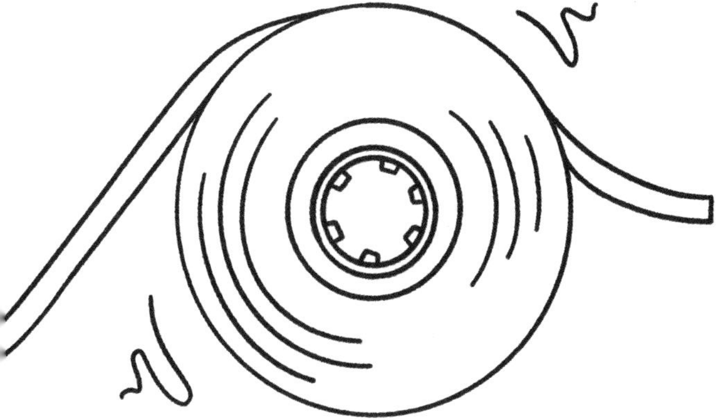

Then, time passes,
and there's less and less
tape left on the reel.
It spins faster."

"Who am I? What is the meaning of life? What am I doing?"

"What is ego, what is mind, nature of mind... and what is desire?"

"I'm just livin', man."

"You go down the river on your independent journey."

"I think vulnerability is probably a key thing."

"Ageing.
I'm just starting to get better at it.
Just the amount of stuff you have
to do before you're dead."

"I wouldn't mind going to outer space."

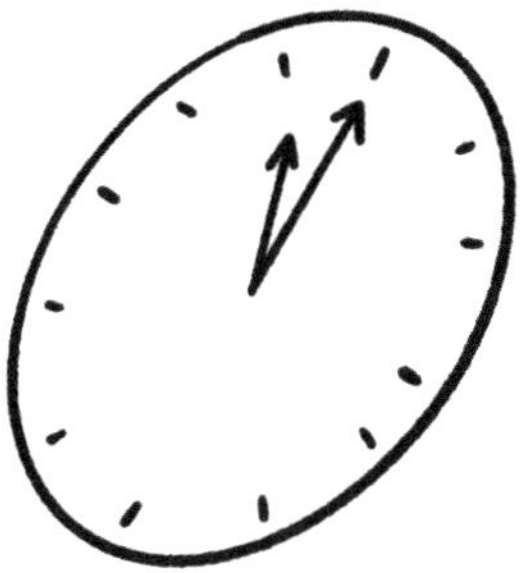

"I only have so much time. I might as well throw myself into the fire."

"I've had wonderful experiences.
I mean really wonderful
[...] Relationships to nature.
Relationships with the self.
With other people."

“You can find love, if you don’t have it.”

"['What do you think happens when we die, Keanu Reeves?'] I know that the ones who love us will miss us."

"Life is precious. It's worthwhile."

SOURCES

BBC,
1998
– pp. **10, 63**

BBC,
23rd July 2024
– pp. **37, 73, 91**

Details,
August 1991
– pp. **23, 26, 27, 58–59, 79, 89**

Esquire,
10th February 2017
– pp. **13, 14, 19, 22, 24, 25, 29, 36, 87**

Esquire,
22nd November 2021
– pp. **11, 33, 34–35, 40, 42, 43, 47, 49, 84**

Fox Studios Sydney opening party,
1998 – p. **62**

Good Morning America,
ABC, 23rd July 2024
– p. **78**

IGN,
19th May 2012
– p. **16**

Inside of You Podcast,
19th December 2023
– p. **86**

Interview Magazine,
11th January 2022
– p. **57**

Interview Magazine,
2nd September 2015
– p. **61**

Magic Radio,
31st October 2024
– p. **88**

Motorcycle Sport & Leisure,
13th February 2017
– pp. **18, 46**

Parade Magazine,
11th June 2006
– pp. **69, 70–71, 72, 75, 93**

People,
28th March 2023
– p. **17**

Rolling Stone,
31st August 2000
– p. **60**

SmartLess,
SiriusXM,
27th March 2023
– pp. **38, 54, 55, 56, 82, 85**

The Guardian,
18th May 2019
– pp. **39, 48, 53, 66, 67**

The Guardian,
19th December 2021
– pp. **15, 32, 50, 51, 52, 80–81**

The Late Show with Stephen Colbert, CBS
– p. **92**

The Telegraph,
2nd November 2024
– pp. **12, 68**

Vanity Fair,
August 1995
– pp. **28, 41, 83**

Vanity Fair,
February 2001
– p. **90**

Quadrille, Penguin Random House UK, One Embassy Gardens, 8 Viaduct Gardens, London SW11 7BW

Quadrille Publishing Limited is part of the Penguin Random House group of companies whose addresses can be found at global.penguinrandomhouse.com

Penguin Random House UK

Published by Quadrille in 2025

www.penguin.co.uk

A CIP catalogue record for this book is available from the British Library

ISBN 9781837833726

10 9 8 7 6 5 4 3 2 1

Managing Director, Publishing: Sarah Lavelle
Publishing Director: Kate Pollard
Senior Commissioning Editor: Kate Burkett
Assistant Editor: Harriet Thornley
Design and Illustration: Double Slice Studio (Amelia Leuzzi and Bonnie Eichelberger)
Production Controller: Sumayyah Waheed

Colour reproduction by p2d

Printed in China by RR Donnelley Asia Printing Solution Limited

The authorised representative in the EEA is Penguin Random House Ireland, Morrison Chambers, 32 Nassau Street, Dublin D02 YH68.

FSC www.fsc.org MIX Paper | Supporting responsible forestry FSC® C018179

Penguin Random House is committed to a sustainable future for our business, our readers and our planet. This book is made from Forest Stewardship Council® certified paper.